Dealing with MOM

how to understand your changing relationship

Dealing with MOM

how to understand your changing relationship

By Laurence Gillot and Véronique Sibiril
Illustrated by Anne-Sophie Tschiegg
Edited by Tucker Shaw

sunscreen

Book series design by Higashi Glaser Design
Production Manager: Jonathan Lopes

Library of Congress Cataloging-in-Publication Data:

Gillot, Laurence.
[Avec votre mère, c'est plus pareil. English]
Dealing with mom : how to understand your changing relationship / Laurence Gillot
and Véronique Sibiril ; edited by Tucker Shaw ; illustrated by Anne-Sophie Tschiegg.
p. cm.— (Sunscreen)
Includes bibliographical references.
ISBN 0-8109-9201-9
1. Mothers and daughters. 2. Parent and teenager. 3. Teenagers—Family relationships.
I. Sibiril, Véronique. II. Shaw, Tucker. III. Title. IV. Series.

HQ755.85.G56 2005
306.874'3—dc22
2004023798

Translated by JMS Books, LLC

AMULET

Published in 2005 by Amulet Books
an imprint of Harry N. Abrams, Incorporated
100 Fifth Avenue
New York, NY 10011
www.abramsbooks.com

Printed and bound in China
10 9 8 7 6 5 4 3 2 1

Abrams is a subsidiary of
LA MARTINIÈRE

contents

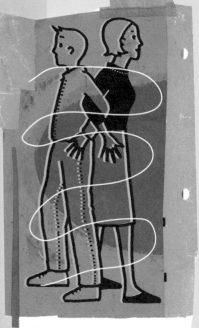

WHY WON'T MY MOM

LEAVE ME ALONE?

WHY CAN'T I TALK

TO HER ANYMORE?

WHAT'S HER PROBLEM?

HOW AM I SUPPOSED

TO DEAL?

Let's face it: there's no one in your life quite like your mother. Although you've been close since the time you were born (and even before), your relationship has changed, developed, and become a lot more (ahem) complicated. But you love Mom and she loves you, so . . . what's going on?

It's all a part of growing up. Like it or not, you're on the fast track to becoming an adult and the way you see the world is changing. You're starting to see your mom as a real person, not a perfect one. You're more questioning, more critical. This doesn't make things easier for you or for her.

So you're finding it a little tougher to communicate with her. Maybe it seems as though she's not really understanding you. You're growing up, making your own choices, and spreading your wings . . . but sometimes Mom makes you feel stuck.

So, what's the deal? And can you deal? And where is she coming from, anyway?

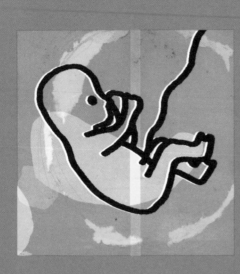

Mom
had a life
before me?

keep it down,
would you?

No one knows
you like
your mom

WAY, WAY BACK IN THE DAY

hey! settle down
in there!

MOTHERS:
CAN'T LIVE WITH 'EM,
CAN'T SEND 'EM BACK

MAKING YOUR
ENTRANCE

mom had a life
before me?

ever dream about having a family one day? Sure, you do. Not that it's going to happen tomorrow or anything, but you've thought about what it might be like to be grown up, to have a home, to have children. And your mother, when she was young, probably did the same thing. She'd daydream about having a little boy or a little girl, maybe even imagine what her children would look like or who they'd grow up to be.

Your mom's imaginary family took a backseat while she grew up. School, friends, travel, work, love . . . all of these were things that, in her own way, she went through. She had times when she was really happy, and times when she wasn't. Just like you, she was sometimes disappointed by the world or mad at her own mother. She had best friends, final exams, shopping sprees, and dating dramas. She spent time wondering who she was and where she was going in life.

sound familiar?

The point is, before she was a mom, she had a life. Which is good to keep in mind when you try and understand what she's talking about and where she's coming from.

when your mom became a
mom

Without getting into the specifics (ew!), your mom and your dad decided to go for it, and *bada-bing*, she was pregnant with you. Whether it was a plan or more of a lucky accident, your mom chose to have you. Or your mom chose to adopt you.

And by committing to being your mother, she gave you a pretty major gift. You have a name, a family, and a permanent spot on the family tree.

Not bad, right?

way, way back
in the day

Believe it or not, your relationship with your mother began long before you were born. So, ____ years ago (you fill in the blank), you and she were really close—as in, you were living inside her. For around nine months you hung out in her belly, and she carried you around everywhere she went.

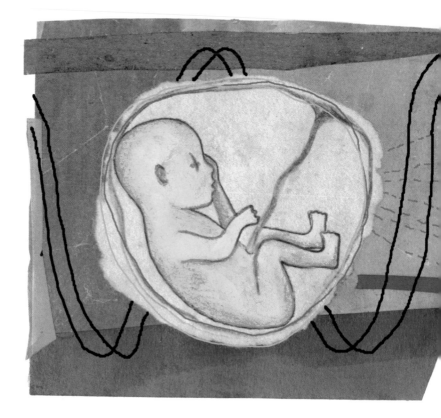

The adventure began when you were just two cells (one from Mom, one from Dad), each with its own special DNA. Together, in these two cells, was everything that would determine your eye color, hair color, height . . . everything about the physical you.

You were only two cells for a few seconds. Two became four, then eight, sixteen, thirty-two, and so on. The cells continued to divide, grow, and develop, and slowly you began to look like a little person. Your body began to move. Your organs began to function. Oxygen and

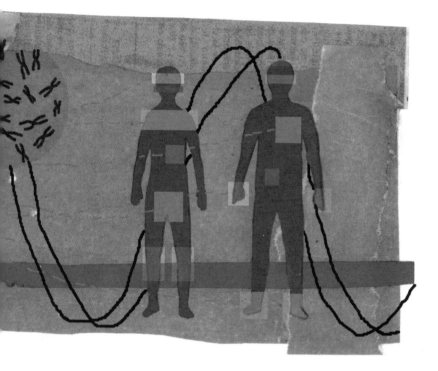

food came straight from your mom, through your umbilical cord. In other words, you relied on her for absolutely everything.

By now you're probably wondering why you need to know all this information, especially in a book about your relationship with your mother. But trust us: it's important to have all the background info you can get. To deal with your relationship now, you have to know its history.

no one knows your mom better than you do...
inside and out

Just because you were stuck inside your mom doesn't mean you were clueless about what was going on out in the world. In fact, you knew what she was up to most of the time. You knew when she was awake, when she was asleep, when she was happy, sad, or totally freaked out.

What's wrong, Mom?

When your mom was stressed out, or late for an appointment, or not feeling so great, you'd hear her heartbeat speeding up. And not only that, your own heart would speed up, too!

Keep it down, would you?

About halfway through your mom's pregnancy, your ears started working. Even though everything sounded muffled and pretty unclear in there (Hello, you were in a womb!), you could definitely recognize your mother's voice. You'd hear the crunch of her chewing, the glug-glug of her digestion, the tick-tock of her heartbeat, and the soft *woosh* of her breath. And if she was laughing, you definitely heard that, too.

Please, Mom, not that George Michael CD again!

In the womb, you were also really sensitive to music, particularly the deep bass sounds. You even had your favorite songs! One study has shown that when pregnant mothers listened to the musical piece *Peter and the Wolf*, their fetuses moved, especially to the low sound of the bassoon. It's also been shown that after they're born, babies smile or gurgle when they hear the same music that they heard in the womb again.

Hey! That tickles!

About halfway through mom's pregnancy, your skin was pretty sensitive. You could feel her stroking you through her stomach.

Pickles and ice cream?

Whatever she ate, you ate. And even though your food wasn't coming through your mouth, the tastes you developed were based on hers. If your mother preferred strong tastes, such as asparagus or garlic, then you probably liked these flavors when you were born. And not only that, but if she smelled something really good—or something really gross—your heartbeat changed.

The deal is this: you spent nine months so totally close to your mother that you can't help being sensitive to her moods, movements, and attitudes. Like it or not, you two are tight.

no one knows you like
your mom

Sure, you were in touch with Mom while you were riding around inside. But she was pretty tapped into what you were up to, too.

Hey! Settle down in there!

Early on in her pregnancy, your mom started to be able to feel you moving around inside. This was a good thing; it meant that you were healthy, active, and growing fast.

You were especially active when she was lying down. When her stomach muscles would relax, it would give you plenty of space to bounce around in there! Somersaults, handsprings, half-gainers with a triple twist . . . you were tumbling harder than the Olympic team.

Your mom, and whoever else touched her tummy during this period, would be able to feel you moving. She'd even be able to tell what position you were in, feeling your heel, your elbow, or your knee under her hand. If she was like most mothers, she'd even talk and sing to you.

Ready for your close-up?

A few times during her pregnancy, your mom probably had the chance to catch a look at you, thanks to a special ultrasound scan. Her doctors used these scans to monitor your health, to make sure you were still healthy and developing normally, and also to record how big, long, and gorgeous you were. As she progressed through her pregnancy, your mom would be able to see your hands, eyes, nose, and toes.

Getting to see you while you were still in the womb gave her all sorts of things to be proud of. She told all of her friends how happy she was that you were coming along so well.

SUSAN

HOWARD

Say my name!

One thing that your mom spent a whole lot of time thinking about was your name. With so many to choose from, and such a big decision to be made, you can be sure she gave it a lot of careful attention and talked about it often!

Maybe she picked the name of a person she admired or liked. Maybe she passed on an important family name. Maybe she chose your name because of its special meaning, such as "Lucy" for light, or "Peter" for strength. Maybe she just liked the way the name sounded, or maybe she wanted something totally original.

But whatever your name is, it is important and meaningful, and you'll have it forever. That's a pretty big decision for her to make!

JONATHAN   ANDREA

making your
entrance . . .

One day, you or the doctor or the midwife decided it was time for you to check out life on the outside. Your birth was exciting, dramatic, exhilarating, and incredibly difficult . . . for both you and your mom. You both felt stress and pain during the delivery, and you were both totally exhausted by it.

Your first moment out, you screamed as you took your first breath. You were tired, grouchy, and confused. Who could blame you? But your mom reached out and the doctor placed you in her arms. She looked you over from top to bottom and memorized your face. You don't remember this moment, but she does, and she always will. It was the first moment she'd really, *really* met you.

She immediately accepted you. And you immediately recognized her—her smell, her voice, her touch. You curled into her breast while she held you close. She talked to you and sang to you. You felt safe with her. And when you were hungry, she let you chow down.

yeah, but when can I get it
pierced?

Just when you thought everything was going to settle down, they picked you up, flipped you over, and waved scissors in your face! It was time to cut the umbilical cord, the fleshy thread that connected you to your mom's placenta, bringing you food and oxygen for the past nine months.

It was an important moment, the "cutting of the cord." After all, it's your first step toward independence. Major!

It's a pretty unforgettable moment for your mom too.

Cutting the umbilical cord also gave you your first scar: your belly button. You'll carry this scar the rest of your life, and while it's just a belly button to you, it's full of all kinds of memories for your mom. Hey girls—maybe that's why she gets all weird when you start talking about the rhinestone belly-button ring you're planning on getting.

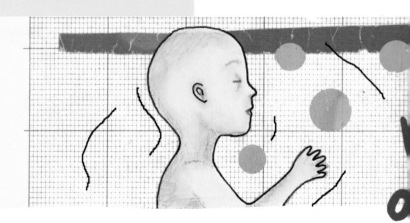

what's your story?

Believe it or not, even before you left the hospital, you already had a history. Your family, your parents, where you lived, how you lived, whether you had siblings . . . all of these factors were part of the setting of the story of your life, and started you down the road to being you. Even though you pretty much did nothing but sleep, eat, cry, and poop, your mom knew exactly who you were—she saw the beginnings of the sparkling personality you have now.

The bottom line? You and your mother were too close, and went through too much together, not to have a special and unique relationship. There's no one on the planet quite like your mother.

IF IT'S NOT ONE THING,

Dad, will you marry me?

HEY, WHERE ARE YOU GOING?

SHAKE WHAT YOUR MAMA GAVE YA!

IT'S YOUR MOTHER!

SEE YA!

Mom, will you marry me?

getting the party
started

So you made it through the stress of being born and finding something to eat, but the truth is, that was only the beginning. As a newborn, you couldn't do anything yourself. You were totally dependent on your mom.

You needed someone to love you, feed you, wash, clothe, and care for you. And although all kinds of people probably pitched in to spoon supper into your mouth or change your diapers, your mother was the one you felt closest to and safest with from the beginning. It's totally normal.

For weeks, she was able to spend hours just staring at you. She felt extremely close to you and protective of you. It even overwhelmed her sometimes. She'd smile, cry, laugh, make faces at you, and cover you in kisses, constantly. She was in tune with what you needed and when, from food to a fresh diaper to just a burst of love, and she was always ready with open arms.

It was during these moments that you really started to get to know each other. You would share moments of joy, moments of sadness, moments of frustration. You'd test each other. You became part of her rhythm of life.

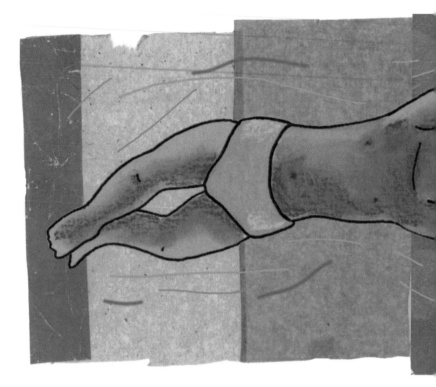

When you were very young, she was often tired and pretty sensitive. She was probably anxious and worried that she wouldn't be a good mother. She wondered why you cried, she panicked when you didn't stop. She freaked about what you'd just puked up, or why you hadn't pooped in two days. She worried that you hadn't had enough to eat, or that she'd drop you.

Like a sponge, you'd soak up her emotions, and when she was bugging, chances are you were bugging, too. But she wasn't the only anxious one. You were pretty freaked out yourself. It took a while for you two to sort each other out and get into a relaxing groove.

Many kids also have another parent in the house: Dad. And as the weeks went on, he started to find his place in the groove you and Mom

had established. You started to recognize him and accept him as part of your crew. And while your relationship with him was unique and exciting, too, you were still dependent on Mom for much more.

When you started to crawl and walk around the playground, you kept her close by. When a dog first barked at you, or when you fell off the swing set, she was the one you called for: "Mom!" You cried when you weren't with her.

But there's no question about it. While you weren't ready to face the world entirely by yourself, you were starting to establish who you were. Your mom encouraged you to be yourself and to love yourself, because she loved you more than anything.

shake what your mama
gave ya!

So you started growing up, feeling more and more independent. First you were feeding yourself, then crawling, then walking, then climbing up and down the stairs. You started babbling, then talking. You

learned how to make your mom smile, and laugh. She was proud, and she loved showing you off to her friends.

She also spent a lot of time just looking at you. Believe it or not, the way your mother looked at you was very important. Her look passed on just as much information as her words, telling you that you were special, loved, and unique.

Which, of course, you are.

boys vs. girls

There was a moment when you were two or three, a moment you probably don't remember, when you realized that there was a difference between your mom and your dad, and it had something to do with what's below the belt.

As far as your feelings for your parents go, this completely confused you.

mom, will you
marry me?

There's this stage of life, around three or four years old, when boys go through this weird phase and fall in love with their moms. Not *really* in love, but they have a strong desire to be the one and only guy in her life. They say things like "I want to marry Mommy," all the time. The only problem? Dad.

It's not like boys want to get rid of their fathers, but they sometimes feel jealous of them; they want to be Mom's one and only guy. But boys eventually figure out that Dad's not going anywhere, and besides, it's kind of nice having him around. And not only that, but some day soon enough, the thought of marrying Mom is appropriately gross. Boys realize they'll grow up and find someone of their own.

dad, will you
marry me?

Boys aren't the only ones who have confusing ideas when they're young. Girls, when they're toddlers, also go through a stage where they fall in love with their fathers. Again, it's not really in love, but they believe they want to be the one and only girl in Dad's life. The only problem? Mom.

In some ways, this period is more complicated for girls, because Mom, who was always your partner and protector, now feels like a rival for Dad's attention. This is why girls often hop in Dad's lap as soon as he sits down or scramble into the passenger seat next to Dad, only to have Mom force them into the back. They volunteer to pass him the tools while he works on the car. They announce "I'm going to marry my daddy!"

The only thing is, no one takes this seriously. Everyone else seems to know that this is never going to happen. Especially Mom. They've seen it all before. And soon enough little girls figure out the deal: Mom is not her rival for Dad's affection. Girls realize that they, too, will grow up and find someone else one day.

hey, where are
you going?

As you grew up, Mom gradually started encouraging you to be more independent. This is a good thing. After all, the last thing you need is to be a baby for the rest of your life. But that doesn't mean it was easy. In fact, separating from your mother, who you used to be a part of, was tough on both of you.

But all kids grow up, and it only makes sense for you to stretch your horizons beyond Mom's hip. At first you were only alone for a couple of minutes at the playground, as you raced across to the other side of the sandbox; then for a couple of hours at a play group; then half a day at preschool; then whole weekends with Grandma and Grandpa.

And while there were times when all you wanted was your mom (you even screamed about it every now and then), you eventually got used to being on your own.

see ya!

By the time you hit grade school, you were used to being around other kids and other adults. You were socializing, joining in, playing well with others, and yes, even fighting. You were learning how to deal in the world by yourself. (Sort of.)

Pretty soon you were asking if you could have dinner at a friend's house, wanting to go to camp for a couple of weeks, and walking home from school by yourself. Then it was after-school clubs, sports teams, and parties with your friends.

Sure, Mom knew where you were pretty much all the time, but you were on your own for hours, days, even weeks at a time. Your universe grew from a playpen to a park to a neighborhood to a city, and while you were psyched for a hug from Mom when you got home, you were also psyched to say good-bye every now and then.

your body is a rollercoaster

MY MOTHER, MYSELF...

I LOVE YOU, BUT BACK OFF!

WHAT'S UP WITH THE WORLD?

Who am I?

Mom,
Is that you?

Mom, do you still LOVE ME?

you have no idea
who i am!

Just when you thought you had your mother figured out, things started getting really confusing. Now that you've hit your teens, you've probably started having more and more difficult moments with Mom. It's not like you're not getting along, it's just that you don't seem to be speaking the same language. It used to be so simple, but things inevitably get more complicated.

For starters, you're not into cuddling with her like you used to. There was a time when a hug, especially when you were mad or sad or even crying, was exactly what you wanted. But now, forget about it. Hugs are annoying, and kisses—even worse.

And can we discuss the constant questioning? The woman is constantly in your business! "How's your friend Charlie? What did you eat for lunch? What did you learn in school? What time will you be home?"

It's not as if you can object to the questioning, because it's not wrong for her to want to know what's up. But that doesn't mean it's not annoying. In fact, it's getting on your nerves, and you start saying stuff like, "None of your business!" or "Leave me alone!"

It's part of being a teenager, an adolescent, and it's not your fault. See, she's still a mom, and still wants to be a mom. And you still want to be a daughter or son. But you're not a baby anymore. Everything feels different.

your body is a
roller coaster

Check the mirror really quickly. See that? Just as you suspected. Your body is changing right before your eyes. Every time you look in the mirror, you see the signs: Hair where there didn't used to be, zits galore, breasts and periods if you're a girl, a deepening voice and constant wet dreams if you're a boy, and stuff like that. All these things come from hormones (progesterone and estrogen in girls, testosterone

and androgens in boys) and they send your body through some crazy changes.

So, if these hormones are doing such a number on your body, you better believe they're doing a number on your brain, too. You're becoming more curious, more intelligent, and more independent. You're emphatic about declaring who you are and what you stand for. And you're standing pretty tall, too.

This makes it a whole lot tougher for Mom to stare you down and say, "Have you finished your homework?" She's speaking to a young adult now and neither of you is sure, exactly, how that works.

crush!

One of the first things you truly feel uncomfortable talking to Mom about, one of the first things that you probably won't share with her, are your first crushes.

There's something about being crazily attracted to someone, in that sudden, immediate, powerful way that only means *crush*, that isn't easy to talk about with Mom. In fact, many teenagers just think it's gross. Even if you and Mom had a frank talk about sex and safety, you probably aren't running to her with all the daydreams you've had about that hottie in math class.

Crushes can be really fun and exciting, but can also throw you into uncertainty, insecurity, and confusion. And the last person you're interested in talking to about it is your mom. In fact, when she asks you about who you're dating and what he or she is like, you just get irritated.

And even when you do try and talk to her, she nails you with an "I understand. I felt exactly the same when I was your age." You want to scream, "No, actually, you don't!"

It's a killer paradox: Mom, who's always made you feel confident and always helped you battle insecurity, is the one person you have the hardest time talking to. You need the confidence only she can give you, but most of the time you two just can't seem to connect.

This is totally normal! It's OK to have some boundaries with Mom. In fact, it's a good thing. But don't shut her out totally. Believe it or not, she might have something useful to say.

your changing view of
the world

So you're taller. You're stronger. And not just that—you're smarter, too. You're sharper, wiser, and way more tuned in to the world around you. You're aware of other people's feelings, not just your own. You're way less childish. You watch how people treat each other. You test out your own ideas and beliefs. You're crushing left and right. You see subtleties and complexities—in your own life and beyond.

But that doesn't mean you've got everything figured out. You're having more experiences and learning more about the world, but in many ways you're more confused than ever.

Only human?

Here is a hypothetical situation: Your parents are divorced, and you live with Mom, not Dad. As a child you just figured, "Dad's bad, he left. Mom's good, she's here."

But now, looking back, you see that maybe it wasn't all that simple. Your dad had strengths and weaknesses, and your mother wasn't perfect, and maybe their breakup wasn't exactly what you thought it was.

As you grow up, you start to see the circumstances in a different way. It may not make you rethink your position, but it helps you see that nothing is quite as simple and clear-cut as you thought. All human beings are complex, and all human situations are complicated. Your parents are exactly that: human.

What's up with the world?

Say what you want about the world out there, but it's never boring. There's always something to grab your attention. Celebrities, fashion, music, religion, war, security, terror . . . you've started watching what's going on, and it's exciting. Scary sometimes, but exciting.

As you've grown up, you've encountered different types of people who live and think differently than you and you've been fascinated. You've also been full of questions.

As exciting as all this new knowledge can be, it can also be confusing. Sometimes you struggle to make sense of it all. What ideas will you adopt as your own? What ideas will you decide aren't for you? Who do you agree with? Who do you disagree with?

What does your mother believe, and do you agree with her?

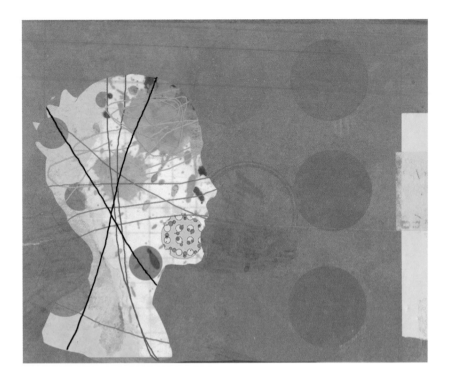

who am i?

The more you learn, the more questions you have. What's in store for my future? What are my strengths? What are my weaknesses? Who are my heroes?

What it boils down to is the one tough question we all face: Who am I? It once seemed like such an easy question to answer: you were a child, your mother's child. But as you grow older, you're no longer defined by your family in the same way. You're a true individual, and will grow into a unique adult.

The question is, who is this adult? And how will he or she relate to your mother?

everyone's crazy!

i can't take it!

You've got the picture. Everything's changing. Your body, your mind...what's next?

Your relationships, that's what. You no longer communicate in the way you used to, and people notice the changes. You're not the same little kid you used to be, and you don't act like it. You feel differently about the people around you, and they feel differently about you.

Your place in the world has shifted from a dependent child to an independent thinker. And this means you've got a challenge on your hands: to communicate and interact with your family like the adult you're becoming.

And it's not just your family that's giving you trouble. You have to readjust to everyone in your life.

Even with your best friends, something has changed. You see them in a new light. They surprise you by acting weird. But they also are the ones who help you understand yourself better. The stranger they act, the more you should remind yourself that they're going through the same things you are, more or less.

Like you, they're trying to define who they are. They do this by watching others speak, live, and act. They also feel tension, confusion, misunderstanding, and frustration. (Especially with their mothers.)

And believe it or not, they're watching you, too. Your friends and peers are emulating you—the way you dress, speak, and think. And you're emulating them. In many ways, your friends are taking over as your role models. When it comes to clothes, music, and even relationships, your friends are becoming even more influential than your mother—Mom just isn't making as much sense to you as she used to. And you'll continue seeking out new role models: athletes, celebrities, teachers, and older friends.

mom,
is that you?

So you've figured out by now that the changes you're going through affect your relationship with your mother. You know her better than anyone, but as you grow older, sometimes she seems like an alien!

Don't worry. Just because you're more grown up doesn't mean your relationship with Mom is a thing of the past. You now have a better understanding of her behavior—not just as a mom, but as a human being. Even when she's acting really strange, you can handle it. (And she

can handle it when you act strange every now and then. And tell the truth, you do.)

Mom knows you're a young adult now, and sometimes she treats you like one. She'll tell you about her long days, ask you your opinion about what's going on in the world, even crack grown-up jokes. She hasn't forgotten that you're her kid, but she's beginning to respect and value you as an adult.

i love you, but
back off!

You still need Mom, but at the same time, you also need your own space. You need time alone, you need your own activities, you need your own friends. When she's always around, it's annoying . . . you want to break free. (Then again, when she's not around, you really miss her.)

When she wants to comfort you, you push her away. (Then again, when she ignores your problems, you get annoyed.) When she questions you about your life, you feel like she's being nosy and intrusive. (When she doesn't ask, you start to think she doesn't care about you.)

It seems like a no-win situation. No matter what she does, it's never quite right. Don't worry, this is normal. It's no one's fault, it's just the way things go with almost every mother and child. Your relationship with Mom is complex and confusing right now, and it takes listening, love, and lots of understanding and patience to make things easier.

get away!
(where are you going?)

By now, you're probably feeling like a yo-yo. You're pushing mom away, but wishing she were around. You need your freedom, but you need your security. You need your wings, but you need your roots. Crazy, right?

Believe it or not, this whole situation has a name. It's called "separation-individuation." (Try saying that twelve times fast.) What it means is that before you become a full-grown adult with your own identity, you have to go through this strange situation with your parents. You have to separate from them, physically, mentally, and emotionally. Especially Mom.

It doesn't happen fast. In fact, it happens very slowly, and sometimes painfully. And it happens in many different ways. Maybe you decide you don't support the same candidates she votes for. Or maybe you decide you're not sure about the religion she practices. You start to wonder about and question pretty much everything she stands for.

It doesn't mean you should totally blow off everything your mom believes. You still have a lot to learn from her. But the cool thing is that she can learn a lot from you, too. Remember, your relationship with your mom takes listening, love, understanding, and patience.

ok, now really
get away!

The need to separate from your mother is something you can't totally control and sometimes you take a stand against her just because you can. It's instinct. And it helps you keep tabs on the fact that she respects you. It's like you're saying "I'm big enough now to make my own decisions and take care of myself," and she's saying, "Well, *OK...*" even though she knows you still need her guidance and love.

She's your mother. She gave birth to you, loved and cared for you, nurtured you, and raised you. She shared her values with you. And up until recently, you went along with her. You accepted her love and nurturing, and you loved her right back, no questions asked.

But as you've grown older, you've started to see that she's not perfect. She has strengths, weaknesses, pluses, minuses. She has qualities you admire and qualities you dislike. She has ideas you agree with and ideas you don't. And opposing her is your way of proclaiming who you are and what you're about. "I'm not a baby! I'm grown up!" (Um, almost.)

Remember, this doesn't mean you don't love her anymore. You still do. In fact, it's only because you care about her so much that these tense times affect you so deeply. No matter how crazy she drives you, she's your mother. It's just that the separation period isn't all that easy on either one of you.

mom, do you still
love me?

Even as you're trying to separate yourself from her and get your own life, you still want her to love you unconditionally. And guess what—she does!

Sure, she doesn't approve of your temporary clip-on belly-button ring, and she's not psyched when you wear torn jeans to school. But she understands your need to express yourself and lets you go for it. If you want to be a vegetarian, she'll help you come up with new dinner ideas while making sure you get the right nutrition; or she may not be an environmentalist as you are now, but she'll clip articles on environmental issues from the paper for you.

Of course, just because Mom loves you and understands the importance of your new camouflage cutoffs, it doesn't mean she's about to cut you slack on everything. For example, that report card better be up to snuff. She'll let you dye your hair four different colors (if you're lucky) but you need to show up on time for class. She encourages you to have all kinds of friends, but forget about hanging with that older boy. She'll give you a curfew, not as a punishment, but as a protection. She knows (and you know, too) that you shouldn't be out all night long.

why can't you be more like

_____'s mom?

Take a look around. How come all of your friends' moms are so much cooler than yours?

Maggie's mother is so young and trendy. Not like yours! David's mother lets him stay out after midnight. Not like yours! Lisa's mom actually hangs out and occasionally lets her drink wine at dinner. Not like yours!

But, get this: Your friends feel the same way about your mom! They look at you and her and they wish their mom was as cool, understanding, and awesome as yours.

mom: as annoying as she is,

you just

Sure, she's annoying and you don't agree with everything she believes. But you really gotta cut your mother some slack. She isn't perfect. (By the way, neither are you.) But she has her good points, and you're lucky to have her.

Believe it or not, she wasn't born a mother, and she didn't know everything about mothering before she had you. She was once a child, and then a teenager, and a student. She was a daughter, a dater, and maybe even a troublemaker. She had boyfriends. She had best friends. She's an individual. Just like you.

Your mom had her own life before you came along, and although you changed her life, she still brings all that experience along with her. Why do you need to know this? Because it helps you understand.

So believe it or not, she has had a lot of the same experiences and emotions that you have. Your opinions sound familiar to her, because she, too, once went through the separation from her own mother that

gotta love her

you're going through. That's when she started understanding what *her* values were, and started defining who *she* was.

Watching you grow up, she sees drama that she recognizes. Believe it or not, she had angsty boyfriends, crazy girlfriends, and painful moments at school. And she also had a first kiss, a prom, a driver's license . . . the list goes on.

Your mother wants you to have the same great experiences she had, but she also wants to protect you from the hardships that will come your way. Sometimes she's right, sometimes she's wrong. She's human.

It's not easy to watch your child grow up, and Mom's not always comfortable with everything. Sometimes she laughs, smiles, and feels tenderness and concern for you. Sometimes she's up all night worrying about your future. It's always something. Even though Mom's in charge, she can't control everything.

For her, your growing up means that you're no longer her baby, and that's not easy for her. She misses the little kid who used to crawl into bed with her after a nightmare.

As Mom watches you grow up, she worries about what's next for you. Who are you hanging out with, what are you not telling her? You grow further away from her, and you need her less, and although that's exactly what you both want (after all, who wants to live at home forev-

er?) it's not exactly easy for her. You don't need her the same way you used to, and this saddens her.

Just like you, Mom's riding an emotional roller coaster. One second she's proud of you and delighted with how well you're growing up. But the next second she misses the little boy or girl you used to be.

All she really wants is a good, respectful, intelligent, adult relationship with you. She wants honesty, understanding, and communication. Sounds a lot like what you want, doesn't it?

you're growing up, she's
growing
older

Get this: the older you get, the older she gets. And this isn't always easy on Mom. Not that she wants to be younger, or go back in time, but she knows she won't live forever, and as you depend on her less and less, she has more and more time and energy to spend on other things.

She looks at her life and remembers her accomplishments. The greatest one is you. But she's more than just a mother. Who else has she been, and who else will she be in the future?

She's spent almost all her time and energy over the past several years raising you (and your brothers and sisters, if you have them).

Sure, she may be a working mom with plenty of other interests, but as her primary interest (you) grows up and prepares to take on the world, she's left with a whole lot more time to think and reevaluate her life.

And although she's happy to have the freedom (you're not the only one who wants to spread her wings!), she's sad, too. She'll miss being a hands-on mother. But she'll make it. Just like you.

my mother,
myself

Among other things, growing up is about defining who you are. The question is, will you be like your mother? Will you model your life on hers? Will you take her ideas and opinions and make them your own? Will you leave behind certain values you don't agree with? How else will your relationship change?

One thing's for sure—you have to keep talking, listening, and expressing yourself in order to understand and be understood. Just like any adult relationship (And yes, you're almost an adult.) this one is based on honesty and respect. Even though she sometimes might be the person you want to talk to the least, it's totally important to keep the communication lines open.

Some people are all about setting up a time each week—maybe at dinner, before your weekly viewing of your favorite TV show—to catch up with Mom. But for most of us it's about chatting while you're doing dishes, while you're in the car, or even on your cell phone. Keeping the communication flowing freely means better understanding—in both directions. It helps remind you, and her, that even if you have issues, you've still got each other's backs.

feeling numb?

HOW ARE YOU

FEELING?

feeling alone?

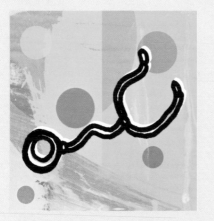

feeling depressed?

FEELING ABANDONED?

feeling ignored?

Stories You Might Be Able to Relate to

FEELING CONFUSED?

mom vs. mom

So far in this book, we've talked mostly about a pretty straightforward, typical situation. We've assumed that the woman who gave birth to you is the same woman who raised you.

But for some people, the situation isn't quite so clear. For many, the woman who conceived and carried you (your biological mother) isn't the same woman who raised you.

Maybe the woman who gave birth to you decided to let another couple adopt you. Or perhaps she died from an accident or illness. Perhaps you live with your biological father and his new partner. Whatever the case, your new mother took you in, looked after you, and raised you.

And she loves you. You probably even consider her your mother, and maybe even call her "Mom."

So when people speak about your mother, you almost want to say, "Which one? The one who raised me or the one who gave birth to me?" It's confusing for you, and your feelings are torn between them.

If your biological mother isn't around, even if she's dead, you may sometimes feel angry toward her (Where is she? Why did she have to leave? Why isn't she here?) and sometimes curious (What did she look like? Would she approve of my family?). You may idealize her when things aren't going well at home, feeling that your life would be better if she were around.

If your biological mother isn't around, your relationship with your family is more complicated. You love your family, including your adoptive mother, but you can't help being frustrated and tense. Even if you never really met her, you miss your biological mother.

It's no one's fault, especially not your adoptive mother's, but you can't help blaming her sometimes for your troubles. You bring up your "real" mother now and then just to remind everyone about your feelings.

It's not fair, and you know it. After all, you may have no idea what your so-called "real" mother is like! Would she be more understanding than your adoptive mother? Maybe, maybe not. Would she be stricter? Maybe, maybe not. Would she be nice? Maybe . . . but maybe not. Sure, she's perfect in your mind, but who knows how she'd be in real life? Both

mothers are incredibly important to who you are.

It's important for you to think about your biological mother. and it's normal for you to idealize her. But the truth is, when it comes to your real life (your grades, your friends, your home), you have to deal with the family you're living with. You have to live in reality, whether it's ideal or not.

As you grow up and get a better understanding of your situation, you're able to see what works.

it's not my fault!

So this is the deal: Whoever is "mothering" you is doing the best she can. She can make you happy some days, angry other days. There will definitely be times when you'll feel like screaming "I never asked to be born! Why doesn't everyone leave me alone!"

It's like this: You're living in this house with these people, and you had nothing to say about it. You have to put up with their rules, live by their habits, and deal with the consequences.

Unfortunately, there are certain things that you just can't change. You're going to have to live with these people for a certain amount of time, and you're going to have to deal with them for the rest of your life. But the big secret is, you have more influence than you think. You can make things better, by staying positive and communicative, and by making yourself part of the family.

Check out the following stories. They may not be exactly like yours, but they might help you figure out a thing or two.

feeling abandoned?

𝓜ary's been living with the Browns since she was three months old. She's always known that her mom and dad are not her biological parents, although it's never really been a problem for her. The Browns have always been incredibly loving and supportive.

But ever since Mary hit her teenage years, she's started to have more questions. Who is my biological mother? Why did she leave me? Wasn't I good enough for her? Didn't she want me?

Mary's confused. She begins to think a couple of things: either her biological mother is a terrible, selfish woman, or else Mary herself isn't lovable enough to get her own mother's love.

Of course the Browns have been reassuring Mary that she is loved, she is lovable, and she's important to them. They explain how Mary's biological mother was unable to take care of Mary, and giving her to the Browns was an incredible act of love and generosity. She knew that Mary would have a better life with them.

But Mary isn't so sure. How can the Browns know what Mary's biological mother was thinking? Why didn't Mary's mother leave her a note, or something to explain what happened?

The more Mary thinks about it, the more confused she gets: Who was my mother? What did she look like? What was she like? If she is alive, does she still think about me? Does she wonder where I am and what my life is like? And my father, who was he? Does he even know about me?

Not knowing the answers didn't used to be such a big deal, but lately, it's upsetting Mary more and more.

Despite all the love she feels from her adoptive parents, Mary feels empty inside. She feels abandoned. And she's afraid that if it happened once, it could easily happen again. After all, if her first mother gave her away, why wouldn't her adoptive parents do the same? Why wouldn't anyone? It's a confusing, frustrating situation.

If you are in the same situation as Mary:

• Keep in mind that you are lovable, no matter what happened with your biological mother. Your new family adores you.

• The fact that you're asking all these questions means that you're smart, thoughtful, and loving.

• Even if you feel confused about where you came from and who your parents really are, you're still *you*, and you're building your own life. Your own relationships (your family, your friends) define you much more than your birth mother does.

• Talk to your adoptive family about your feelings. Maybe it makes sense for you to learn more information on your birth mother. If so, you can work with your adoptive family to find out more.

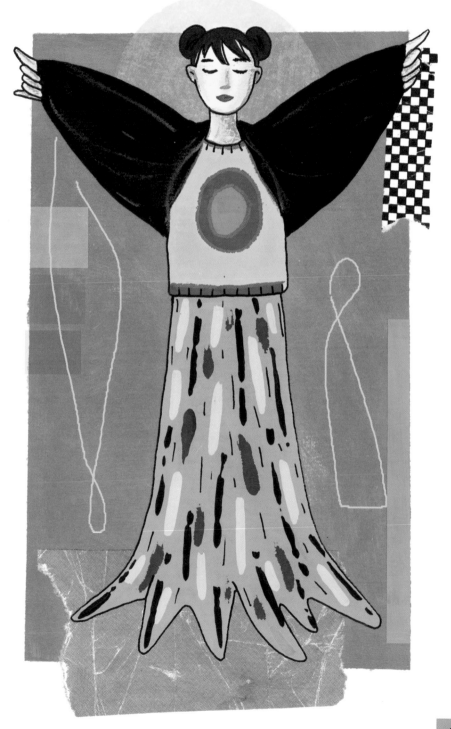

feeling numb?

Martin had a great life and enjoyed his loving parents until just about a year ago. There was a terrible car accident . . . a sharp curve, a blinding rainstorm, and a tree. Instantly, Martin's mother was killed. She was only forty-two.

Ever since that day, Martin's been numb. He cannot feel anything. He thinks the world is an evil, dark place, and he walks around in a daze. It's like he's had something amputated, like a part of him is missing. He's angry, sad, frustrated, and afraid. Why did she have to die?

Sometimes, he's even angry at her for not being there, for leaving him alone in the world without a mother. He knows it wasn't her fault, but he can't help feeling this way sometimes.

As the days go by, things don't get easier for Martin. Each morning, he wishes she was there to help him get ready for school. Each night, he wishes she was

kissing him good night. She was always there, always taking care of everything, from his grades to his health to his happiness. He misses her smile, her cooking, her love. He even misses getting yelled at.

And not only that, but Martin's father is a mess now, too. The man whom Martin thought was stronger than anyone in the world is sad, quiet, and removed.

If you are in the same situation as Martin:

• If you're not getting help from a therapist, get help. You need to find ways to understand what happened and put together some plans for the future.

• Allow yourself to cry. You're in an incredible amount of pain. There's nothing wrong with being sad about losing a parent. It's important to express your pain. Cry!

• Talk to your friends, to your father, to anyone you trust.

• Keep your mother alive, even though she's passed on. She's still there in your thoughts and memories, and she still warms your heart. Don't lose that. Her memory may confuse you sometimes, but it can be a source of great strength. Your memories of Mom don't begin and end with the accident. There's more to the story, and it's your job to keep that story alive.

feeling alone?

Gregory's mom has breast cancer. She's in pain, she's weak, she's suffering. Her treatments leave her exhausted and she's lost a lot of weight. She tries to take an interest in Gregory's day-to-day life: his math test, his tennis game. But no matter how hard she tries to participate, the pain is sometimes too much. And for Gregory, it's chaos. His whole life was turned upside down the day she was diagnosed, and nothing's been the same since.

Gregory does his best to help out. He looks after his kid sister, making sure she brushes her teeth and ties her shoes. He helps Dad carry home the groceries, and even pitches in to help make dinner. Gregory is proud that he's able to make a difference. It makes him feel important, like an adult.

But sometimes, it angers him. If Mom was healthy, Gregory would be able to spend more time with his friends. He wouldn't have to take the bus to school, she'd drive him. He wouldn't have to try and make the waffles that only Mom knows how to make.

And to see his mother, the one who took care of him for so many years, in so much pain is incredibly difficult.

Gregory's totally worried. What if Mom doesn't get better? What if she dies? What if she's not there to listen, to advise, to protect him? Will Dad be able to handle it? Would they ever survive as a family if she passed on?

Gregory cries and worries, but he also does stupid things. He shoplifts. He acts up in school. He picks fights. He does all of these things because he's decided not to care about anything. After all, why should he behave? Behaving isn't going to change his situation at home.

Gregory feels alone and has no clue who to talk to about it all. His sister is too young and needs him to be strong. His dad is more and more distant and stressed. His friends don't really understand what's going on. His teachers scare him . . . after all, he's been slacking off in class and he's afraid they're just going to yell at him about his GPA.

But Gregory doesn't care about the future. Why should he? He can't care about something that he can't even imagine.

If you are in the same situation as Gregory:

• Talk about it! If you don't feel that you can confide in your friends or family, get Dad to help you find a therapist or someone to talk to about things. It should be someone who knows a thing or two about illness.

• Remind yourself that you're not responsible for your mother's health or happiness. No matter how much you help out, you can't cure her. But you can love and support her and that's as helpful as any treatment out there.

• Keep talking to her. Ask her about her illness; ask her how she's feeling. Tell her about your life, about your day. As sick as she is, she still wants to know what's up.

• Keep on living! Keep up with your friends, read books, stay on top of what's going on. The last thing she wants is for you to put your life on hold while she's healing.

feeling depressed?

When Julie gets home from school, she finds her mother at home, in the dark, just sitting in a chair.

"What's up?" asks Julie.

"Nothing," says Mom, flipping the channel on the TV.

It's been weeks since Mom's been herself. She doesn't do much these days, doesn't say much, doesn't go out much. She wears sweats, she doesn't look after herself, and doesn't wear makeup like she used to. She spends less time than ever cleaning up. And meals are mostly frozen pizzas or takeout. Mom just doesn't seem interested in what's up in her life.

Julie's aware that her mother's not well. Mom is stressed, worried, and acting strange. When this episode first started, she and her father tried really hard to keep Mom busy and keep her energy up. Julie tried to keep her own troubles to herself and not talk to Mom, not wanting to worry her even more. She tried to be cheerful and stay positive, telling Mom all about her day, about what was up with her friends, about the

shopping trip she'd just made to the mall. She even skipped going out a few times to stay home with Mom, thinking she'd keep her company.

But then Julie's dad started giving up. He was leaving for work early and staying late. He tried to be kind and attentive, but he wasn't really tuned into what was going on. It was as if he tried, but only to a point. His final answer was to bail out.

This frustrated Julie. All she could say was, "Mom! Snap out of it! You can't just sit around like this, day after day, just moping around!"

Her mother broke down, sobbing. She had no answer for Julie.

This bummed Julie out, big time. She felt like a bad daughter. She was helpless, and she didn't understand why. Why couldn't Mom just snap out of it?

Julie went from concerned to freaked out to worried. She wondered what her mother needed to get better. Drugs? Therapy? Just more love? She never knew what kind of state she'd find Mom in—sad, manic, spacey, or what.

More and more, Julie went from worried to straight-up angry. "What about my life?" she thinks. "This depression is ruining everything!" She begins imagining a different mother, one who's energetic, excited about things, and loves to laugh.

If you are in the same situation as Julie:

Having a mother who's depressed is incredibly difficult for everyone around, including you. You're worried, and unhappy, and probably ticked off that she's not snapping out of it. After all, she's supposed to be the mother, not you!

Here are some things to keep in mind to help you cope:

• Help her out but be careful not to take on too much. You can't do everything for her. She must maintain some responsibilities. It's important for her to do things for herself.

• You are not responsible for her condition. Remember that.

• She's depressed, not you.

• You are not her parent. You're still a kid.

• Remind her that she's important to you, and that you love her. Even if she doesn't seem to understand, or it doesn't feel like she loves you back, she does. Tell her you'd like to help her help herself. Ask her if she's made an appointment with a doctor. Tell her it's important to you.

• Depression can take on many different forms and effect people in different ways. Talk with an adult whom you trust about the situation. Even if he or she can't solve it, he or she can listen, and that helps.

• Even though Mom's going through a rough patch, it doesn't mean she wants you to put your own life on hold. Keep up your friendships, keep up your grades, keep up your life!

feeling ignored?

Leslie suspected something was up. Mom wasn't quite her normal self lately. She'd been looking in the mirror more, wearing more makeup, coloring her hair. Leslie even overheard her telling a girlfriend on the phone about all the new hip clothes she had bought. Mom was in

a great mood, smiling a lot, and her voice changed when she talked on the phone. Soon enough Leslie figured out what was up: Mom was in love!

For a moment, Leslie thought this might be OK. But before long, Leslie was more worried, suspicious, and angry than excited.

"She's always busy now," complains Leslie. "She never pays any attention to me, and forgets things that I've told her. It's like she only thinks about herself."

The other night, Leslie was in her room doing homework when Mom swept in wearing a new dress. "How do I look?" she asked. "Don't wait up. I'll be out late!" She left Leslie at her desk and took off.

Leslie was annoyed, even angry. "How can she just run off like that? Aren't I the one who should be dating? What gives?"

If you are in the same situation as Leslie:

So there's a new man in your mother's life and you feel like every-thing's different. You think, "Wait a minute, we've got a good family unit going on. Why is everything changing? Is Mom unhappy with the way things are?"

• Don't panic. This new guy isn't going to get in the way of you and your mother any more than the new person you're dating will get in the way. There's no competition here. You'll always be your mother's kid, and no new guy is going to get in the way of that.

• Remind yourself that if it were a friend who'd found a new man, instead of your mother, you'd probably be more supportive and encouraging. Try and use those feelings here.

• Your mother is human. Therefore, she has the capacity to be in love. In fact, she loves being in love. This is a good thing!

feeling
confused?

For the last several years, Jeremy has lived with his mother and Claire, his mother's partner. Jeremy has had a terrific childhood with a lot of love, laughter, and joy. He never felt that he was missing out, and the three of them had a great time together.

Sure, his friends sometimes said stuff like, "Which one is your mom?" and "Why don't you have a dad?" but Jeremy never thought too much about it.

But for the last few months, Jeremy's started to think more about what's up. "Where is my father? Why does everything have to be different for me? Why can't we be like every other family?" Nothing's changed at home, it's just that Jeremy's been growing up, and starting to wonder more.

He's frightened, too. Once he hit junior high, the comments from his friends suddenly got a whole lot meaner.

Mom and Claire have noticed. They, of course, know that their family is unique. And for them, as adults, it's easy to make sense of it. But

Jeremy and his friends are having more trouble. Even though he knows better, he starts telling people that Claire is just his aunt who's staying with them for a while.

So he's conflicted. He loves Mom, and he loves Claire, and so far everything's been normal. But he's confused, and angry. Why can't he and his family be like the families of all the other kids at school?

If you are in the same situation as Jeremy:

• When your family is different, whether it's gay parents, a single parent, older parents, or whatever, it's harder to stay strong when others make comments. But keep in mind that even though your family is different, it's strong, loving, and stable. That's a lot better than a lot of your friends' families.

• Remember who you're talking about. They're your parents, they love you! It's OK to love them back, even if they're different from most parents.

• Be willing to talk to your gay parents about the situation. Trust that they've given it a lot of thought.

• Allow yourself to have your own point of view about it, but remember to respect your parents' decisions and choices, just as you'd want them to respect yours.

• Feel free to ask questions about your father, and listen carefully to how your mother explains things. It's important for you to know your history!

• Remember that if you have gay parents, it doesn't mean that you're gay, too. You'll have your own path to travel, no matter what the deal with your parents is.

• Look at your situation as an asset. Your unusual family means that you've had more experiences than most people, that you've seen sides of the world that many people never see. Add these experiences up, and you'll see that your life is richer, and you are wiser for it.

suggestions for further reading

Books

. . . any advice?
By Fiona Gibb and Tucker Shaw
(Puffin Books, 2000)

*Deal With It! A Whole New Approach to Your Body, Brain,
and Life as a Gurl.*
By Esther Drill, Heather McDonald, and Rebecca Odes
(Pocket Books, 1999)

GirlWise: How to Be Confident, Capable, Cool, and in Control
By Julia Devillers
(Three Rivers Press, 2002)

Web sites

Alloy.com

Cosmogirl.com

Gurl.com

Teenlineonline.org

Index

A